# Man's Best Friend

ISBN 978–0-9823291-1-5

# Man's Best Friend

## John G. Murphy

White Lightning Publishing

Malibu, CA

# *INTRODUCTION*

When I put out my first poetry book "Spirit's Flight," I had a friend say she was looking forward to a poetry book on dogs and with a dog's perspective. So Krys, this one is for you. However, not all are from a dog's view.

I have always had a love for dogs and I guess to some degree it shows up in my writing. Dogs have played a large part in my life even from way back as a kid. I can remember just being 7 years old and sitting on the porch steps of the old farmhouse. I was sitting there with a few pups around, talking and singing to them. Just basically hanging out with them. Even as a young teen, I had a Chocolate Lab named *Sugar* that I spent many days out in the Appalachian Mountains hiking with her through the woods. We would run the creeks and in the winter time, and I would take my skates along to skate the creek. It was a good time for me considering I was living in a trailer in the sticks with no running water and for a time no electricity. My time out in the woods with the dogs were blissful for me.

# *CANINES*

You know in my life I've had all kinds of pets

But for me, there is one kind that stands out among the rest

They're quite content when they are being used

And their love doesn't fail even when they are abused

The word that describes them best, is loyalty

Loved by the poorest and even by royalty

No, there is clearly something that sets them apart

Something so special it can warm a cold heart

Often a better companion to man than man

I am just one of many, who is a big fan

They are able to do so many things

They can sniff out a bomb or help with drug stings

They're always around when you're feeling sick

Or they will entertain you by fetching a stick

Clearly they are the truest friend to man

Yes, I am a dog person and proud that I am

# A BIT OBSESSED

Come on, come on, come on, please

If I could, I'd get down on my knees

I know that you know what I need

If you throw it, I'll bring it back in God's speed

Having to wait here just seems so wrong

I have been waiting here for far too long

You see that stick to me, is like your favorite song

And me running and fetching it, is where I belong

I realize I seem a bit obsessed

But if you throw it, I'll feel so blessed

I'll return it as long as this heart beats in my chest

And will forever think, that you are the best

# CHIHUAHUA

Hey, what's the big idea?  Do you think I like being small?

Do you think if I could've chosen, I would've chosen to be tall?

I don't like being down here with all of you giants around

With all your big, floppy feet trying to put me in the ground

I know some seem to think that I am mean

But to tell you the truth, it's all a big scene

It's mostly a show I use to get by

Really in truth, I'm a very nice guy

You see, I'd get walked on if I don't put on this face

It is hard for a Chihuahua to survive in this place

So excuse me if I come off a bit rough

But life being this small can sure be tough

# *FOR AS LONG AS I REMEMBER*

For as long as I remember, dogs have been in my life

And I'll have them until I die, so I told my wife

She is not the dog fan that I tend to be

But dogs have always been so very special to me

One of my first memories is climbing in a dog house

I slipped in so gently; as quiet as a mouse

You see, our dog had just given birth to a bunch of pups

They were so cute and tiny, they would fit in teacups

I think my folks were worried because I was only three

But the momma dog was fine, I think my love she could see

I didn't try to pick them up; I just laid right down beside

The affection I had for those pups, I just could not hide

I believe I stayed right there until I fell asleep

A wonderful childhood memory I always wish to keep

And so I plan, right up until the end

To always have a dog, my companion, my friend

# GROOMED

What on Earth makes you think this is fun?

I'd rather be at the park, or out for a run

All this poking and pulling, I think is kind of nuts

Do you have any idea, what they did to my butt?

No, this grooming thing is way overrated

The smell from the last time, has just barely faded

Yeah, I suppose the groomers are nice enough

However, the last gal was kind of rough

What's so wrong with smelling like scat?

If she touches my paw again, I'm going to snap

Wait until she's done, spraying with that hose

I'll shake so hard, it will be dripping from her nose

I do like when I'm done ,and you make a big fuss

And now that it's over, it wasn't that tough

I especially like that you let me on the bed

Before morning's light, I'll be sleeping on Dad's head

However, before too long, you will have me groomed

And I'll most likely act, like I am positively doomed

# HER TRUE FRIEND

He was so faithful, tried and true

In so many ways that she only knew

The way I grew up, I couldn't understand if I tried

The way it tore her up and the way that she cried

I guess you felt you had lost a true friend

You had to know it would eventually end

You know you have had a truly true friend

When both of you have made it to the very end

Yes, truly good friends are hard to come by

I guess I am learning why it is that you cry

You were there for his first day but not his last

I am sure he wished you were there when he passed

I know you say there will  never be another like him

I wonder if there was, would you even let him in

I hope you don't miss it while thinking of the past

Something special that could last and last

Yes, let your guard down for a possible new start

Maybe another might bless your heart

Isn't it funny the way dogs touch people's hearts

Try to describe it, I can't even start

Maybe it's the way they're so giving inside

Or the loyalty they have and just can not hide

What is it that makes people feel for them so?

They are the best friends to man that I know

# K9 ANGEL

How I wish I was home

It feels like I am all alone

Well, not alone, you are with me

You're so warm lying by this tree

Your warm hair feels good on my skin

I'm so glad I am here with him

I wish that I had not gotten lost

My nose bitten by a bitter frost

All kinds of noises I hear tonight

The kind that surely give me a fright

Oh, the night can be so cold

Especially when you're only six-years-old

Hey now boy, why did you bark?

Is something scaring you in this park?

No, I don't like this, not one bit

You're scaring me now; come here and sit

I wish you could tell me what you hear

If there is something we need to fear

Hey there boy, I hear something too

Someone is coming to our rescue

I can't wait to see Mom and Dad

And tell them of the night we had

I'll tell my folks that I never cried

For you were with me, by my side

# LEFT BEHIND

Yee-haw, he picked up the keys

I can almost smell the ocean breeze

Or maybe we'll go play at the park

Sorry, I couldn't contain my bark

Wait, why are you leaving me behind?

This is not at all what I had in mind

Oh man, I hate it when he does this

Sitting home thinking of all I will miss

All I can do is count the hours until he's home

Maybe I should just go chew on my bone

Of course, that leather couch looks divine

Bet he would think twice before leaving me behind

He could have taken me out to empty my bladder

Guess I'll pee on the cat and watch her scatter

I can't believe he didn't leave me something to eat

He will be lucky if he has any shoes for his feet

Of course, if he fed me, I would have to go

He knows how I love the grass in the bedroom so

Wait, I'm so excited he is finally coming home

Now wait a minute, I can smell he is not alone

You know what that means, I'll be kicked out of bed

When she comes in, maybe I'll bite her on the leg

Hey now, she seems kind of nice

If she keeps scratching my ear, I might have to think twice

# MAN'S BEST FRIEND

I heard a story where a dog saved his master

Keeping him from a most certain disaster

A man pulled a gun and was going to do him harm

The Golden jumped up and grabbed hold of his arm

Yes, the pup was a hero that very day

But hero or not, he would have done it anyway

I heard of a dog that so loved his child

He stayed beside him when lost in the wild

At night, he curled up and kept him warm

He stood by him to keep him from harm

When he heard help coming, he let out a bark

Because of him, the child made it out of the park

There are many dogs that will lay down their life

They will take on a lion, a bear, or a man with a knife

They don't seem to mind dying for their master

I hope there is a place for them in the hereafter

A dog is selfless and doesn't put up a fuss

They are the perfect example for all of us

A dog, a dog, oh what a gift

A dog is always there when you need a lift

A dog is loyal when loyalty can't be found

He's even there when you don't want him around

He's humble, faithful, tried and true

If you have a dog, oh lucky you

# NAMING YOUR PET

You need to be careful what you name your pet

For what you name them, you just might get

Name them "Trouble" and it's what they'll be in

Call them "Barker" and they will get under your skin

"Bonkers" is a dog's name that comes to mind

If he lives up to it, a new house he might find

I think "Precious" is a good name for a dog

Or "Mr. Clean" you could call your pet hog

"Lovey" would be good for a Siamese cat

A loving Siamese, can you imagine that?

I don't think you should name a Pit Bull "Killer"

Or a Neapolitan Mastiff something like "Thriller"

No , it seems they grow to their  name

As if somehow it is life's little game

So if you are thinking of a name for your pet

Think of what you name them, you might get

You  might think it is an oxymoron

But unfortunately, this you can rely on

Yes, be careful in choosing a name

For you might get  exactly the same

One-Eyed Jack

# ODE TO LIGHTNING

It was a rough start for that little white guy

While performing a C-section, the vet tossed him aside

The pups were to large and the delivery went wrong

Doc said they went without oxygen for way to long

She picked up the white pup and said, "No, not this one.

He's going to be special and shine like the sun"

Picking him up, she rubbed him like crazy

She said "He's not dead, he's just being lazy"

She got him revived after a short little while

I am telling you what, it sure made her smile

In his first year, he was a gangly little thing

He looked so funny the first time in the ring

When in his prime, he looked really fine

I would walk him around, proud he was mine

Little did I know, I think he felt the same way

We were truly best friends until his dying day

He became so popular, everyone knew who he was

I just held the leash, but he was the buzz.

I'm not saying that little white dog was perfect

He messed up because he didn't know the rules yet

He would run off like he'd been shot from a pistol

But if I wanted him back, I just had to whistle

He was a friend to everyone at the county pet fair

He would sit there for hours without ever one care

People would pet him and he would play with their kids

He could draw in a crowd with the noises he did

Now, there were times he did have his days

Every once in a while, he'd show his ornery ways

One day I came home, leaving my lunchbox on the floor

Lightning was smart and knew what it was for

He opened it up and ate all my hot jerky

Poked a hole in my soda, I guess he got thirsty

When I walked in, I saw candy wrappers on the floor

I yelled for the kids as I slammed the back door

It turned out it was not their fault at all

It was that potbellied pup, leaned up to the wall.

There was a little girl he always knocked down

She'd be so excited to see him and leave with a frown

Then there was the time I made a hard left turn

He flew out the window and got a bad brush burn

I stopped the van and opened the driver door

He hopped up inside and looking like "What'd you do that for?"

Oh, and the time I tried to get him to chase a bunny

He ran right over top of it; I just thought that was funny

He never did see that bunny hiding away

I still get a chuckle out of it when I think of it today

I know you're thinking he is just a dog, and you're right

But he brought so many smiles, that little white light

Yes, there were some times that were not his shining glory

But I tell you the truth, they make the best stories

Yes, he was the best of man's best friends

He was tried and true right up to the end

Now I am sure many of you have stories like this

But if you don't, I hope you see what you've missed

A house is not a home without a dog of your own

Go out and get a good dog so you're not alone

White Lightning was a dog

But not your average dog

He was a little white Staffordshire Bull

Man, I am telling you, he was cool

He would do anything he could do for you

He was dedicated, loyal, truer than true

He had a smile that could light up your world

Or he could get ugly if you messed with his girl

# SONNY

Sonny was a good boy; I should have never let him go

It's always when they're gone that you finally know

But unfortunately then, it's just way too late

Time and destiny has somehow sealed your fate

So now I'm left wondering how he is

Wishing I had another dog with a temperament like his

Sonny was a Pit Bull and loyal to the core

I never had to worry if a stranger came to the door

If you were in the family, he had much love inside

But if you meant any harm, you better run and hide

Good luck with that, he was faster than any man

And he had that attitude that always said "I can"

He despised coyotes and always kept a watchful eye

He never caught one, but always gave a good try

One coyote escaped diving though a barbed wire fence

Sonny plowed right through, it was quite intense

He came home with a few marks on his chest

With a big smile on his face, he was the best

Because we had to move, I had to let him go

In a small apartment there was no room for him to grow

He got a great new home, but we didn't stay in touch

Just letting him go was really way too much

I wonder about him and what he's been up to

Sonny, I wonder if you know that I'm missing you

# *SCRUFFY*

As I walked along my way

I found a scruffy little mutt, that rainy day

He was cold and in need of suds

His hair was tangled and full of mud

I stuffed him in my coat, I'm not sure why

It might have been the twinkle in his eye

That little guy was so ugly; he was cute

He turned out to be so very loyal to boot

# OLD FRIEND

I'll see you later my old friend

I'm so sorry your time has come to an end

I'll miss our leisurely walks in the park

Or when wanting to play, the way you barked

So many things are going to change

And life without you will be quite strange

I'm going to miss having you around

When I was cooking, you could always be found

You never let a scrap hit the floor

You looked so cute just begging for more

Yes, I'll miss the times when you just lay near

I would reach over and scratch your ear

Yes, I hope there is a place for you upstairs

I hope you're with someone who cares

I picture you as you frolic and play

The way you did in your younger days

Until that time when we meet again

Goodbye for now, my dear old friend

9 780982 329115